Dandelion Launc[hers]

Reading and Writing Activities
for Units 11-15

PhonicBooks

www.phonicbooks.co.uk   Enquiries@phonicbooks.co.uk
Tel: 07711 963355   Fax: 01666 823 411

Contents

Unit 11: ck, wh

Unit 12: ng, qu

Unit 13: ch

Unit 14: sh

Unit 15: th

Notes on Dandelion Launchers Workbooks

Dandelion Launchers Workbooks contain a variety of multisensory activities and games linked to the stories in the Dandelion Launchers reading scheme. The activities are designed to help develop the skills underlying fluency in reading and writing.

To become a reader, a learner needs to acquire the skill of pushing together individual sounds to make a word. This process is referred to as 'blending'.

To spell words accurately, a learner needs to be able to break a word up into its component sounds. This process is called 'segmenting'. The learner can then write the letters that represent the sounds in a word.

The activities offered will develop blending and segmenting skills in a fun and accessible way for the younger child.

The workbooks also include activities for letter formation, developing expressive vocabulary through retelling the stories and first comprehension exercises.

Clear instructions for every activity appear at the bottom of each page.

Dandelion Launchers Workbook Units 11-15

Dandelion Launchers Workbook Units 11-15 is divided into five units or levels.

Each unit is based on four reading books from the corresponding unit in the Launchers reading scheme.

Books in Units 11-15 introduce the concept that two different letters can represent one sound. For example, in Unit 11, the two letters c + h represent one sound 'ch' as in 'ch i p'.

Unit 13 introduces the spelling <th>. The spelling <th> can represent two different sounds: 'th' as in 'th i n' and 'th' as in 'th i s'. There are lots of activities in the pack to support this new learning.

Some of the activities in the pack can be done before reading the books and others after reading them. This systematic approach helps the reader to enjoy success at each stage and will motivate them to continue learning.

Each activity has instructions at the bottom of the page to ensure understanding. Some Units include reading nonsense words. It is useful to practise reading these words as they encourage the skill of blending sounds into words. It also prepares the reader for reading words with more than one syllable in which the syllables have no meaning until they are combined into a whole word. e.g. 'rel ish'.

The progression in this workbook is as follows:

Unit 11:	ch
Unit 12:	sh
Unit 13:	th
Unit 14:	ck, wh
Unit 15:	ng, qu

Planning your lessons

These suggestions will help parents and teachers use the activities in this pack to reinforce and support reading development.

1. Lessons should be offered daily, when possible, and not last more than 15 minutes initially with younger children.

2. The activities in this pack support the important new learning that two different letters can represent one sound. For example, c+h represent one sound 'ch' as in 'ch i p'. Unit 13 also introduces the spelling <th> which represents two different sounds: 'th' as in 'th i n' and 'th' as in 'th i s'. This pack provides a variety of activities to support these important stages of learning.

3. Model segmenting words into sounds, and blending sounds into words orally. Encourage the reader to point to the spellings (graphemes) as they sound out the words. Make sure that the reader is matching the sounds in the words to the spellings on the page when reading and spelling. If the reader is missing sounds, indicate where this has occurred in the word.

4. Word building and missing sounds activities should precede reading the books. Story telling, comprehension, handwriting and dictation activities follow reading the book.

5. Try to make the lessons as much fun as possible, using the games in the pack to reinforce and support new learning.

6. Always ask the child to say the sounds and push them together to read new words when playing a game. The teacher or parent should model this for the child and do the same when playing.

7. Continue to reinforce the appropriate use of capital letters. Draw children's attention to them where they are used in the activities. Encourage them to find capital letters in books, comics and signs when reading.

Some tips for your lessons

- Lessons should be exciting and fun.

- Give plenty of praise and encouragement.

- Provide small amounts of new learning in each lesson.

- Provide lots of opportunity for rehearsal.

- Make lessons as multisensory as possible, involving the senses of touch, sight and speech.

- Hand success back to the child. If a child reads a word incorrectly, provide them with the missing information so that they can blend the sounds and read the word themselves.

- Use letter sounds, not names.

- Make sure you do not add extra sounds to a sound i.e. 'm' 'a' 't' and not 'muh' 'ah' 'tuh'.

- Encourage the learner to sound out words when reading, writing and playing games.

- Use games as a way to provide needed rehearsal of new learning. Each one of our books has a game at the back which can be photocopied.

Dandelion Launchers

This book belongs to

PhonicBooks

www.phonicbooks.co.uk   Enquiries@phonicbooks.co.uk
Tel: 07711 963355   Fax: 01666 823 411

Dandelion Launchers tick chart
Units 11-13

Unit 11 'The Big Chip'

Unit 12 'Shep and Tosh'

Unit 13 'This and That'

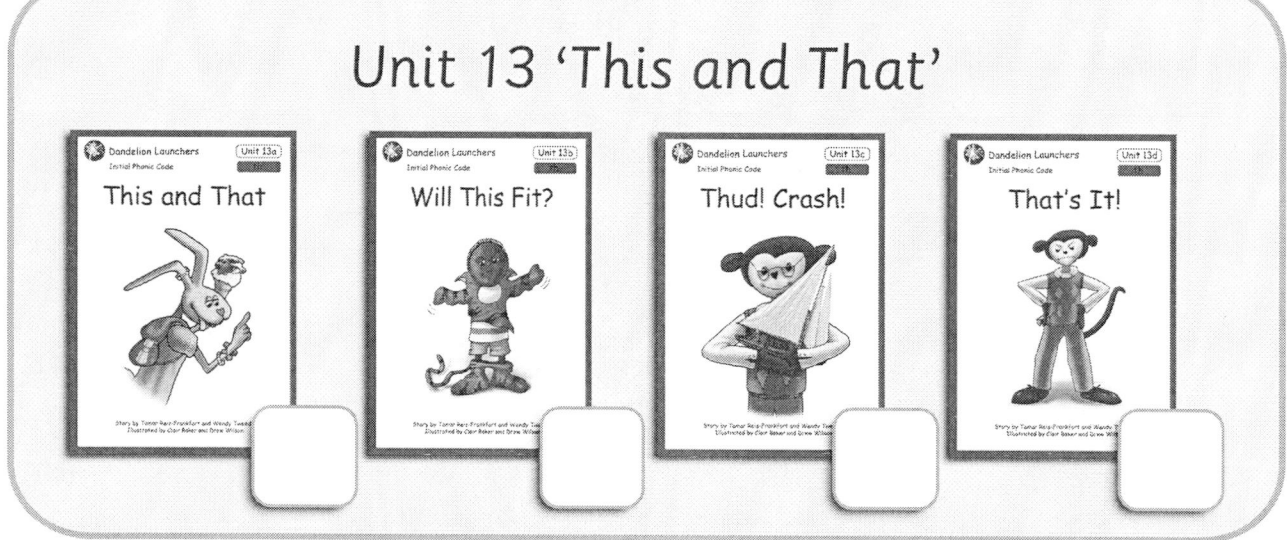

Dandelion Launchers tick chart
Units 14-15

Unit 14 'The Clock'

Unit 15 'Ding, Dong!'

Reading and Writing Activities

Unit 11

Game for Books 11a - 11d: ch

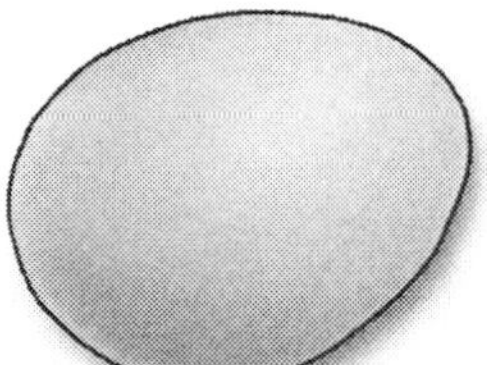

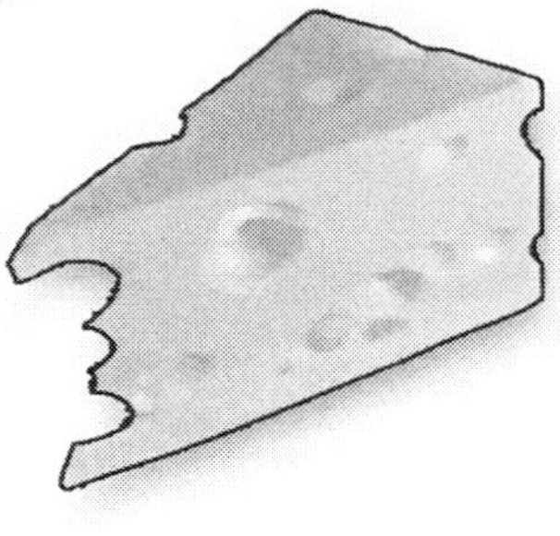

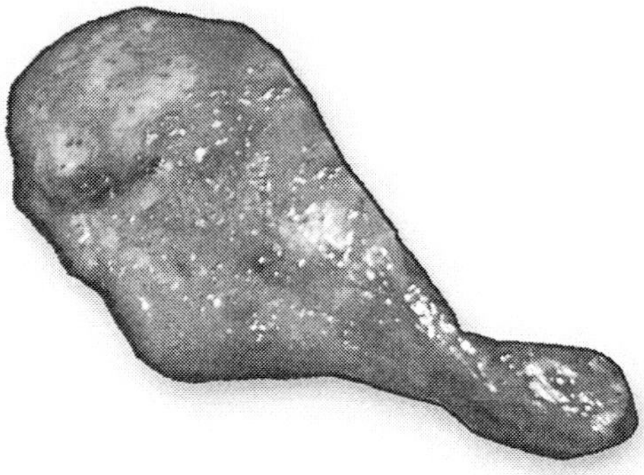

Lunch
Box

Cut out the foods beginning with 'ch' and put them in the lunch box.

Book 11a - The Big Chip Game: ch

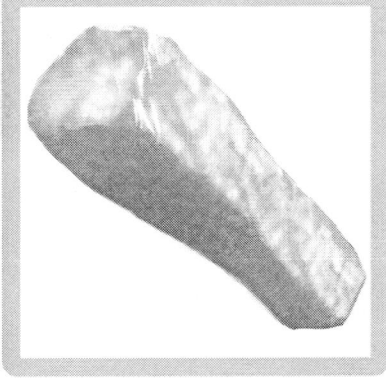
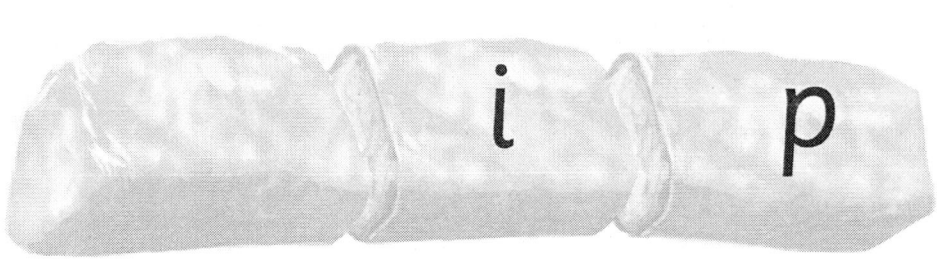

i p

b e n

l u n

Can you fill in the 'ch' sounds on the chips to build these words?

Book 11a - The Big Chip Game: ch

 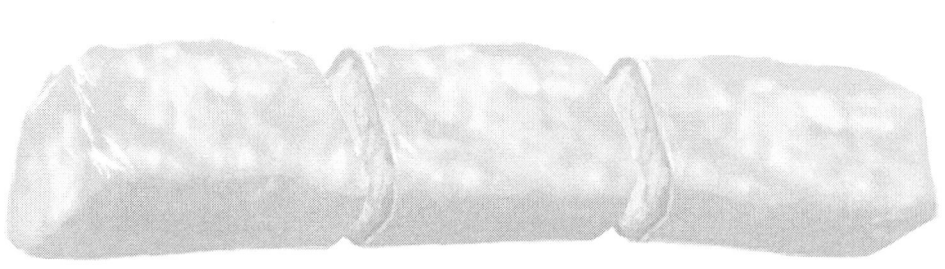

 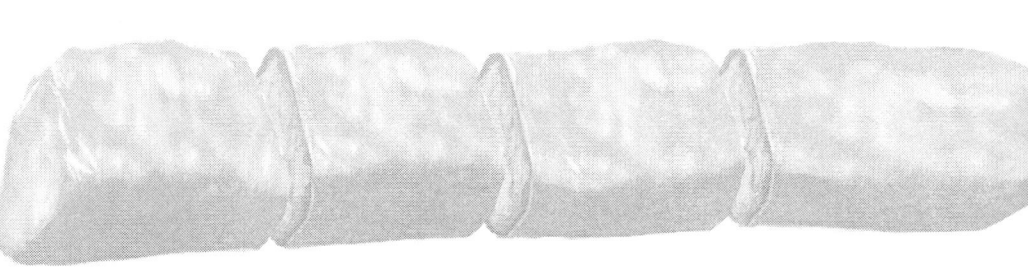

 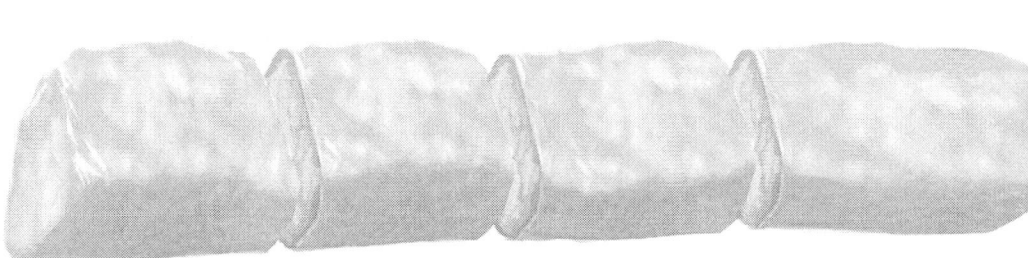

Can you fill in the missing sounds on the chips to build these words?

Book 11a - Retell the story

'The Big Chip'

This page can be photocopied onto card. Cut out these pictures for retelling the story or for children to make their own story. Can also be used to reinforce vocabulary.

Book 11a - Comprehension

The kids tug on the chip.

"It is such a big chip," says Ken.

Ken chops the chip up in to bits. Yum!

Ken and his pals sit on the log and chat.

Cut out the sentences. Read and match to the correct pictures.

Book 11a - Sentence dictation

" _____ _____ is _____ _____ _____ a _____ _____ _____

_____ _____ _____ ," says _____ _____ _____ .

Offer the sentence below as dictation. Encourage the children to sound out the words as they spell them.

"It is such a big chip," says Ken.

Book 11a - Free writing

Free writing with picture cues. This page can also be used for sentence dictation using sentences from the book.

High-frequency words: his, the, a, to, is, my, say, I, says

Book 11a - Sentence handwriting

Ken and his pals

sit on the log

and chat.

Ken chops the chip

up in to bits. Yum!

Book 11b - Chit Chat: ch

ch

pun

ess

ben

lun

imp

op

Sam is saying lots of words with the 'ch' sound in.
Use the 'ch' card to see whether the 'ch' sound goes at the beginning or end of the word.
When you have decided where it goes, write in the 'ch' to finish the word.

Book 11b - Retell the story

'Chit Chat'

This page can be photocopied onto card. Cut out these pictures for retelling the story or for children to make their own story. Can also be used to reinforce vocabulary.

Book 11b - Comprehension

But Sam is not in bed.
Sam gets the chess set.

Dad naps on the bench.

The kids get in to bed.
Dad sits on the bench.

"Get to bed," Dad says,
"and no chit chat!"

Cut out the sentences. Read and match to the correct pictures.

Book 11b - Sentence dictation

the _____.

Offer the sentence below as dictation. Encourage the children to sound out the words as they spell them.

Dad naps on the bench.

Book 11b - Free writing

Free writing with picture cues. This page can also be used for sentence dictation using sentences from the book.

High-frequency words: to, says, no, is, the

Book 11b - Sentence handwriting

Dad runs in.

"No chess! Get in

to bed."

Dad naps on the

bench.

Book 11c - 'Nuts for Lunch': ch

Stan has iced some cookies with words with the 'ch' spelling in.
Can you colour in the ones that have a real word on them?

Book 11c - Retell the story

'Nuts for Lunch'

This page can be photocopied onto card. Cut out these pictures for retelling the story or for children to make their own story. Can also be used to reinforce vocabulary.

Book 11c - Comprehension

Such a lot of nuts!

"Have a nut for lunch!" Stan said to his chums.

"Let's plant a nut next to the bench," said Stan.

Stan gets a nut for his lunch.

Cut out the sentences. Read and match to the correct pictures.

Book 11c - Sentence dictation

a

_____

for   his   _____ .

Offer the sentence below as dictation. Encourage the children to sound out the words as they spell them.

Stan got a nut for his lunch.

Book 11c - Free writing

Free writing with picture cues. This page can also be used for sentence dictation using sentences from the book.

High-frequency words: a, is, to, the, for, his, I, have, said, plant, of

Book 11c - Sentence handwriting

Stan had a chest.
It is next to the bench.

Stan got a nut for his lunch.

Book 11d - The Champ Game

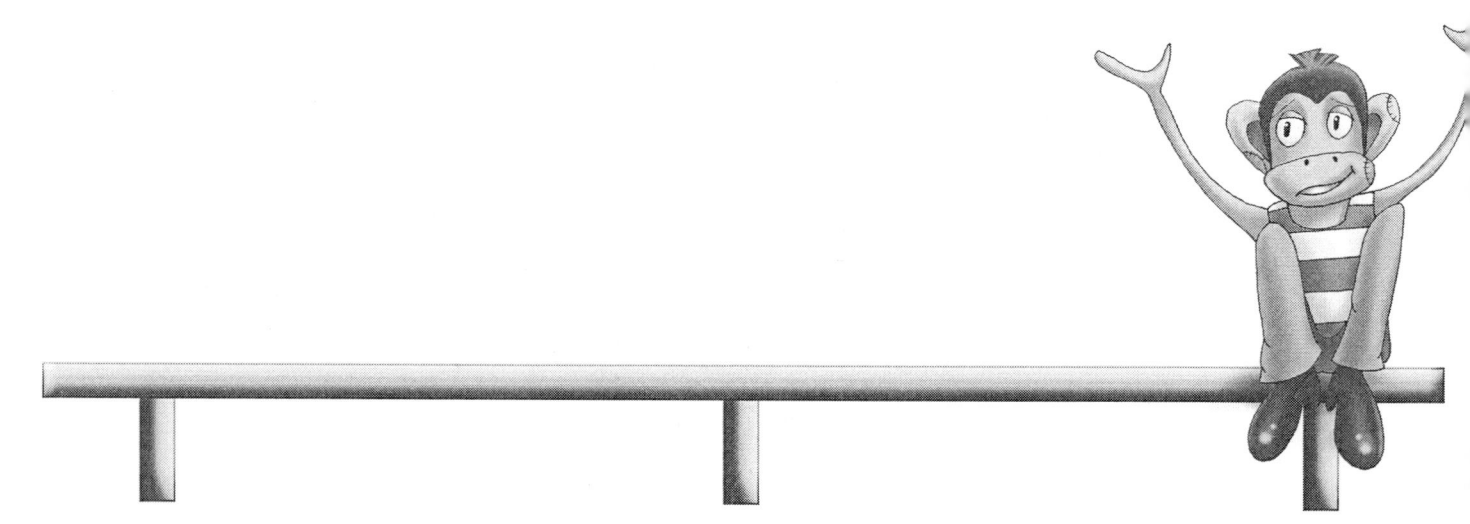

Chimp is collecting cups with real words on.
Can you cut out the cups with real words on and put them on his shelf?

Book 11d - Retell the story

'The Champ'

This page can be photocopied onto card. Cut out these pictures for retelling the story or for children to make their own story. Can also be used to reinforce vocabulary.

Book 11d - Comprehension

Chimp is a champ!

"I can skip!" says Jill. "I am a champ!"

The branch snaps! Help! Chimp grabs a branch.

Chimp jumps from branch to branch. He is a champ!

Chimp is sad. He is not a champ.

Cut out the sentences. Read and match to the correct pictures.

Book 11d - Sentence dictation

and _____ a branch.

Offer the sentence below as dictation. Encourage the children to sound out the words as they spell them.

Chimp runs off and sits on a branch.

Book 11d - Free writing

Free writing with picture cues. This page can also be used for sentence dictation using sentences from the book.

High-frequency words: the, is, says, a, is, he, branch, to

Book 11d - Sentence handwriting

Chimp is sad.
He is not a champ.

Chimp runs off
and sits on a
branch.

Word handwriting

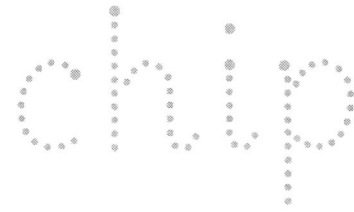

Unit 11 - 4-in-a-row Game : ch

The Champ
Nuts for Lunch
Chit Chat
The Big Chip

chip	chat	bench	chop	want
chess	such	chin	much	lunch
chit	chest	chum	bench	punch
chum	munch	rich	chomp	pinch
lunch	chill	bunch	champ	much
chip	punch	chap	chimp	chest
bench	chat	pinch	chum	bench

Play with two sets of coloured counters. Two players take turns to read the word and put a counter on the word. The winner is the first to get four of his or her counters in a row. The winner places a counter on a chocolate bar. The game is played four times until all the chocolate bars are covered.

Word-building and spelling list

chat

rich

chop

much

bench

munch

pinch

chest

lunch

champ

A list of words from this Unit to be used for spelling practice. Photocopiable cards for word-building are included at the back of the workbook.

Reading and Writing Activities

Unit 12

Book 12a - 'Shep and Tosh': sh
Word reading practice

Shep is wishing for lots of things with the 'sh' sound in. Can you match the word cards to the pictures? Sound them out as you read them.

| dish | brush | fish | ship | cash |

Book 12a - 'Shep and Tosh': sh
Fill in the missing sounds

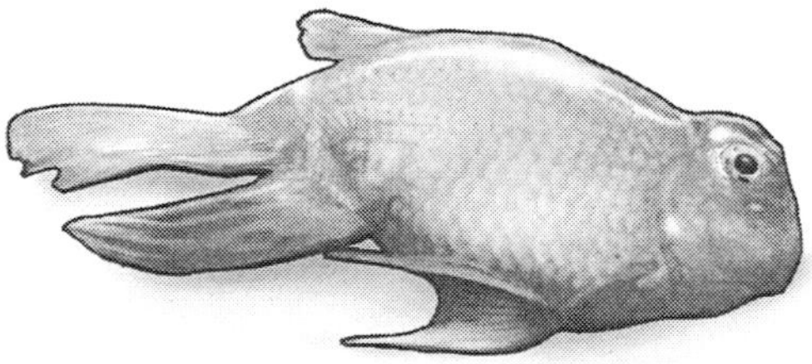

_ _ _ _

_ _ _ _

_ _ _ _

_ _ _ _

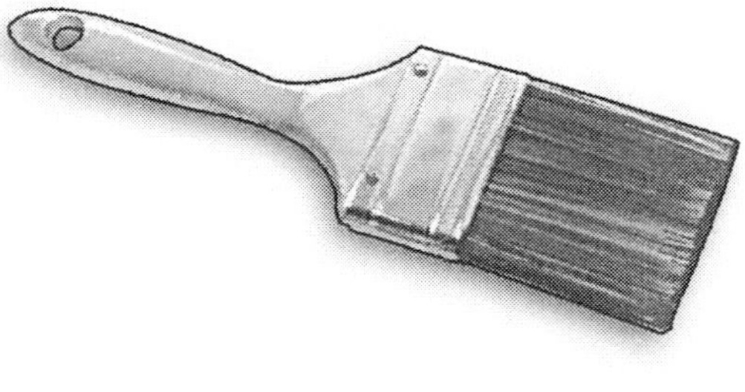

_ _ _ _

Shep is wishing for lots of things with the 'sh' sound in. Can you write the words underneath his wishes? Sound them out as you write them.

Book 12a - Retell the story

'Shep and Tosh'

This page can be photocopied onto card. Cut out these pictures for retelling the story or for children to make their own story. Can also be used to reinforce vocabulary.

Book 12a - Comprehension

| Shep ran and hid in a shrub. | The big dog yelled at Shep. |

| Shep ran to a big dog. | "Will you be my pal?" said Tosh. |

Cut out the sentences. Read and match to the correct pictures.

Book 12a - Sentence dictation

was   a _____ .

_____ a _____ .

Offer the sentences below as dictation. Encourage the children to sound out the words as they spell them.

Shep was a big dog. Shep had a wish.

Book 12a - Free writing

Free writing with picture cues. This page can also be used for sentence dictation using sentences from the book.

High-frequency words: I, a, was, you, be, my, to, no, yelled, said

Book 12a - Sentence handwriting

Shep was a big dog.
Shep had a wish.

Tosh was not a big
dog. Tosh had a
wish.

Book 12b - The Shop: sh

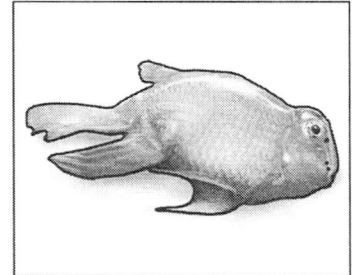

Josh has a shelf in his shop for all the things with a 'sh' in. Can you cut them out and stick them on the shelf?

Book 12b - Retell the story

'The Shop'

This page can be photocopied onto card. Cut out these pictures for retelling the story or for children to make their own story. Can also be used to reinforce vocabulary.

Book 12b - Comprehension

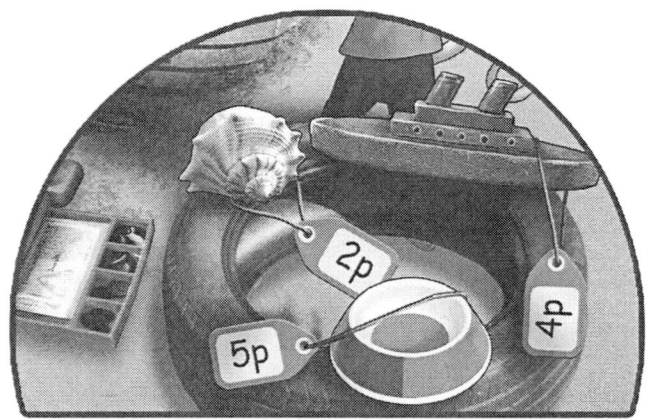

Mum gets buns from the shop.	Josh sets up a shop. It has a till.
Josh sells the buns and gets lots of cash.	The shell is 2p. The ship is 4p. The dish is 5p.

Cut out the sentences. Read and match to the correct pictures.

Book 12b - Sentence dictation

the   .

Offer the sentence below as dictation. Encourage the children to sound out the words as they spell them.

Mum gets buns from the shop.

Book 12b - Free writing

Free writing with picture cues. This page can also be used for sentence dictation using sentences from the book.

High-frequency words: the, a, has, is, I, have, asks, of

Book 12b - Sentence handwriting

Josh sets up a shop. It has a till.

Sam and Tam rush off. Josh is sad.

Book 12c - Fresh Fish: sh

jesh

shoff

rash

shop

shup

fresh

gesh

shim

splash

shut

Can you help Bob find all the fish with a real word on them?
Draw round them when you find them.

Book 12c - Retell the story

'Fresh Fish'

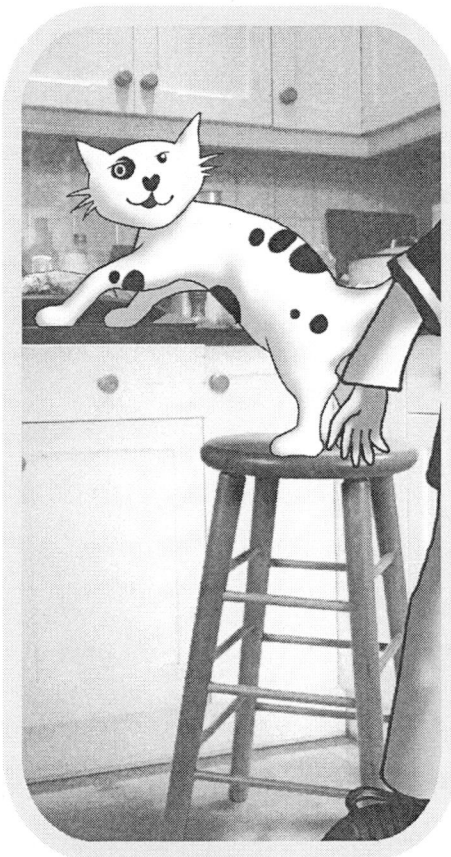

This page can be photocopied onto card. Cut out these pictures for retelling the story or for children to make their own story. Can also be used to reinforce vocabulary.

Book 12c - Comprehension

The fish is on the dish. Dad gets a pan.

"The fish is fresh," says the man in the shop.

Bob can smell the fish in the dish.

The fresh fish is in the bag.

Cut out the sentences. Read and match to the correct pictures.

Book 12c - Sentence dictation

the

the   .

Offer the sentence below as dictation. Encourage the children to sound out the words as they spell them.

Bob can smell the fish in the dish.

Book 12c - Free writing

Free writing with picture cues. This page can also be used for sentence dictation using sentences from the book.

High-frequency words: is, the, says, a, to

Book 12c - Sentence handwriting

The fresh fish is in the bag.

Bob can smell the fish in the dish.

Book 12d - The Fish Pond

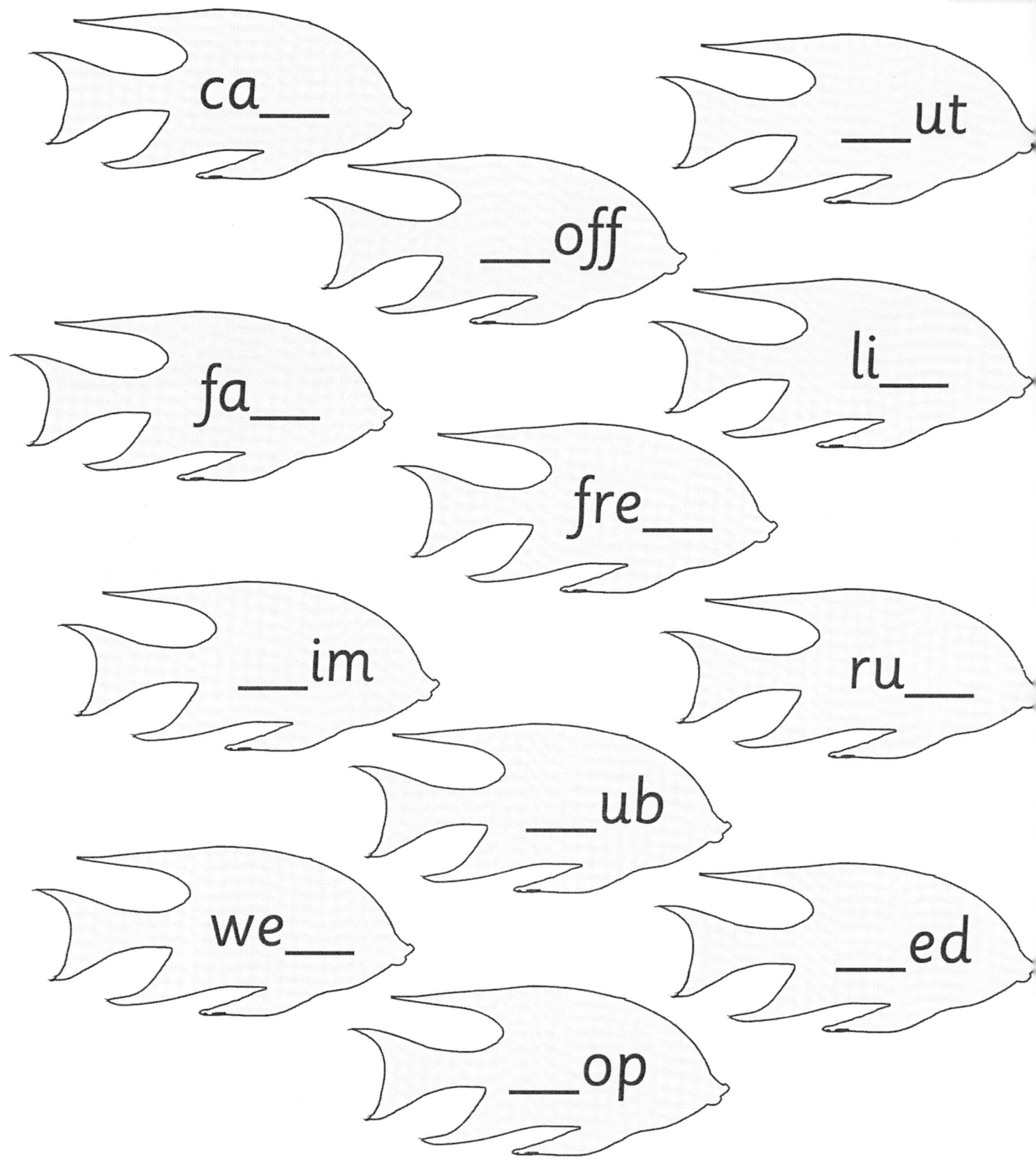

ca___

___ut

___off

fa___

li___

fre___

___im

ru___

___ub

we___

___ed

___op

The 'sh' sound has washed off these fish. Can you write it in and read the words? Colour the fish that have a real word on them.

Book 12d - Retell the story

'The Fish Pond'

This page can be photocopied onto card. Cut out these pictures for retelling the story or for children to make their own story. Can also be used to reinforce vocabulary.

Book 12d - Comprehension

Bob hid in the shrub.

Bob sat next to the fish pond.

Bob jumped in to the fish pond. Splash!

The fish swam off. Bob is glum.

Cut out the sentences. Read and match to the correct pictures.

Book 12d - Sentence dictation

!   The

.

Offer the sentences below as dictation. Encourage the children to sound out the words as they spell them.

Splosh! The fish swam off.

Book 12d - Free writing

_____

_____

_____

_____

Free writing with picture cues. This page can also be used for sentence dictation using sentences from the book.

High-frequency words: the, to, my, said, jumped, no, for

Book 12d - Sentence handwriting

Bob sat next to the fish pond.

"Fresh fish on my dish. Yum!" said Bob.

Word handwriting

shrub

shop

fresh

fish

Unit 12 - 4-in-a-row Game : sh

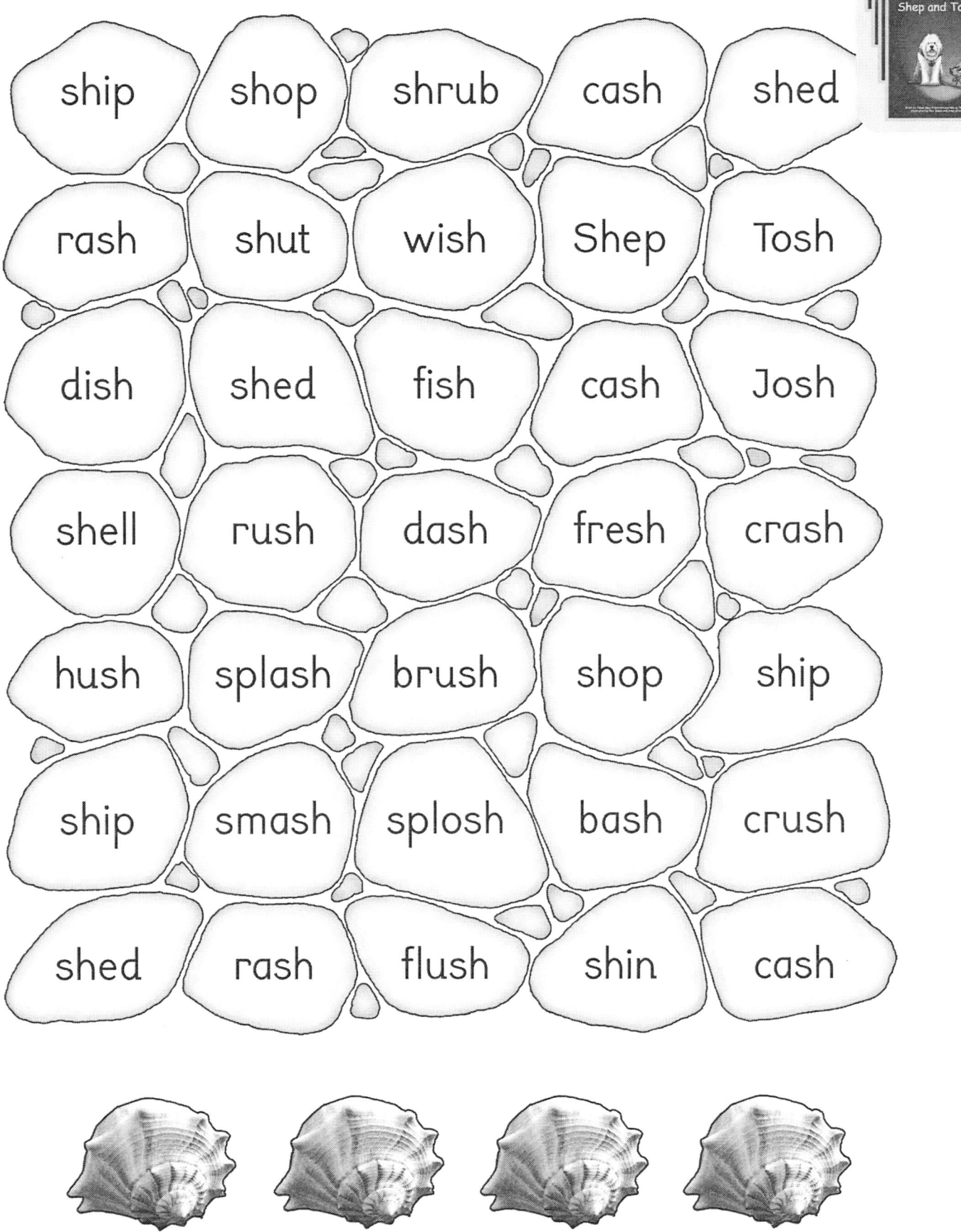

ship   shop   shrub   cash   shed

rash   shut   wish   Shep   Tosh

dish   shed   fish   cash   Josh

shell   rush   dash   fresh   crash

hush   splash   brush   shop   ship

ship   smash   splosh   bash   crush

shed   rash   flush   shin   cash

Play with two sets of coloured counters. Two players take turns to read the word and put a counter on the word.
The winner is the first to get four of his or her counters in a row. The winner places a counter on a shell.
The game is played four times until all the shells are covered.

Word-building and spelling list

ship

shop

cash

rush

shed

crash

shrimp

flush

splosh

fresh

A list of words from this Unit to be used for spelling practice. Photocopiable cards for word-building are included at the back of the workbook.

Reading and Writing Activities
Unit 13

Book 13a - 'This and That': th

m o __

b a __

c l o __

p a __

A moth has eaten the words off the labels on this cloth.
Can you fill in the sounds to write the words?

Book 13a - 'This and That': th

A moth has eaten the words off the labels on this cloth.
Can you fill in the sounds to write the words?

Book 13a - Retell the story

'This and That'

This page can be photocopied onto card. Cut out these pictures for retelling the story or for children to make their own story. Can also be used to reinforce vocabulary.

Unit 13a - Comprehension

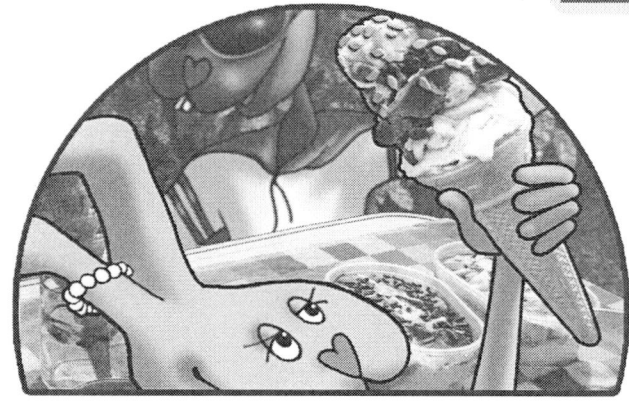

Beth went to Alf's shop.

and this on top..."

"Can I have this...

"I think that's it.
Thanks. Yum!"

Cut out the sentences. Read and match to the correct pictures.

Book 13a - Sentence dictation

"I _____ ___ ___ _____ ___ ___ ___"

"_____ . ___ ___ ___ ___ . _____ ___ !"

Offer the sentences below as dictation. Encourage the children to sound out the words as they spell them.

"I think that's it. Thanks. Yum!"

Book 13a - Free writing

Free writing with picture cues. This page can also be used for sentence dictation using sentences from the book.

High-frequency words: to, I, have, a, of, the

Book 13a - Sentence handwriting

"I think that's it.
Thanks. Yum!"

"Can I have this
and a bit of that?"

Book 13b - 'Will This Fit?': th

mo

at

em

in

is

pa

th

The 'th' spelling has fallen off these party ice cream words.
Cut out the 'th' and try it at the beginning and end of the words to see
which real words you can make.

Book 13b - Retell the story
'Will This Fit?'

This page can be photocopied onto card. Cut out these pictures for retelling the story or for children to make their own story. Can also be used to reinforce vocabulary.

Unit 13b - Comprehension

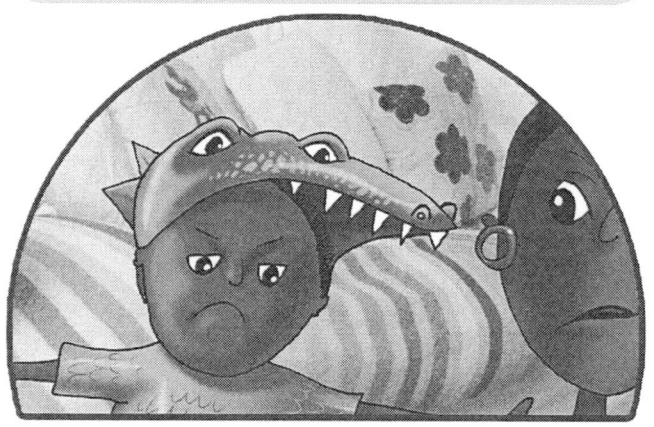

"This is the best!"
says Fred.

"And will this fit?"
Fred thinks.

"That will not fit,"
Mum says.

"Will this fit?"
Fred asks Mum.

Cut out the sentences. Read and match to the correct pictures.

Book 13b - Sentence dictation

" _____ _____ _____   _____ _____ _____   _____ _____ _____

_____ _____ _____ ," _____ _____ _____   says.

Offer the sentence below as dictation. Encourage the children to sound out the words as they spell them.

"That will not fit," Mum says.

Book 13b - Free writing

Free writing with picture cues. This page can also be used for sentence dictation using sentences from the book.

High-frequency words: asks, says, a, she, is

Book 13b - Sentence handwriting

85

"That will not fit," says Mum.

Mum gets a big, red cloth. "This will fit," she says.

Thud! Crash!

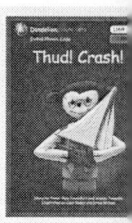

Book 13c - Thud! Crash!: th

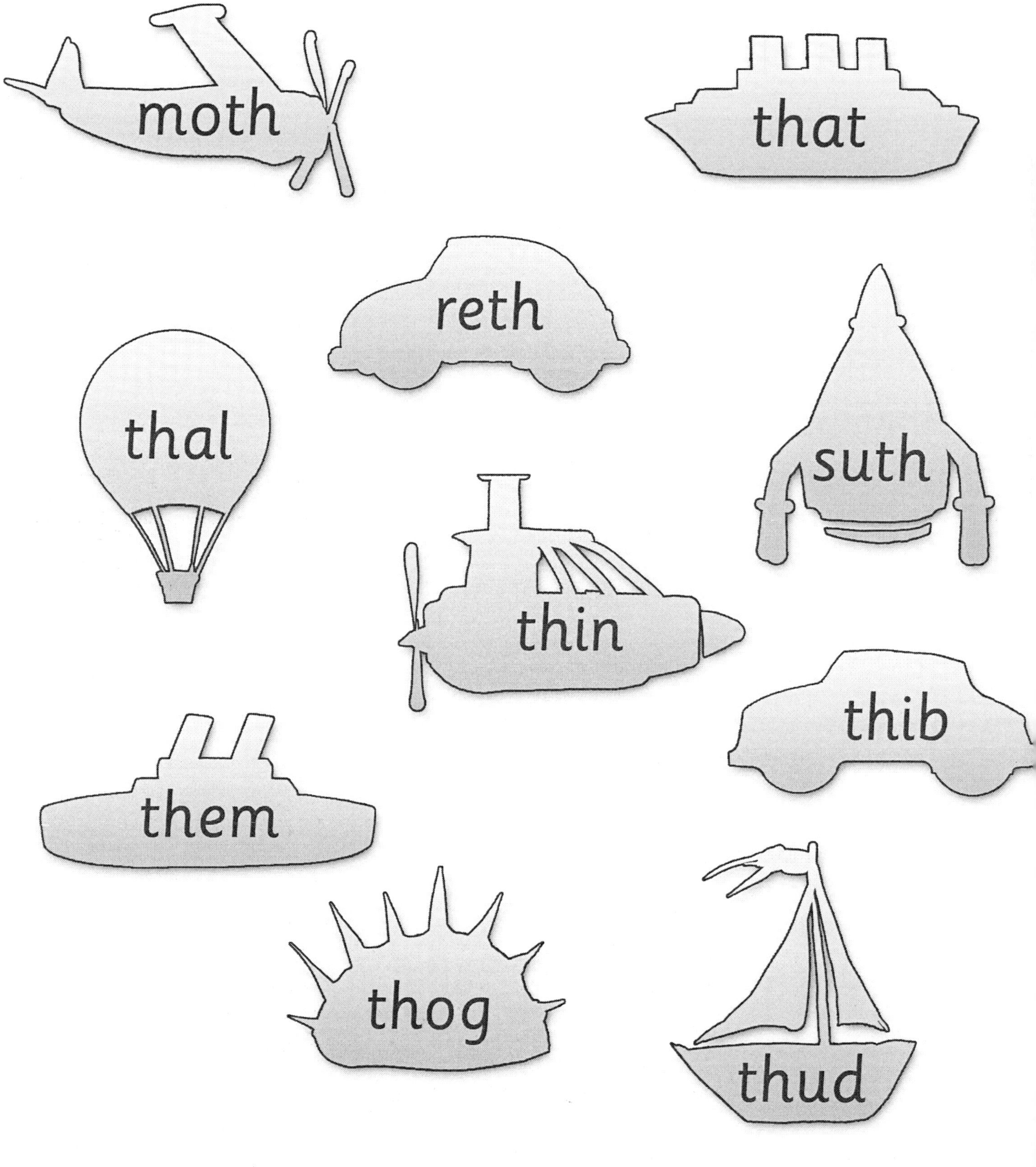
moth
that
reth
thal
suth
thin
thib
them
thog
thud

Colour the models with real words on in one colour.
Use a different colour for the non-words.

Book 13c - Retell the story

'Thud! Crash!'

This page can be photocopied onto card. Cut out these pictures for retelling the story or for children to make their own story. Can also be used to reinforce vocabulary.

Book 13c - Comprehension

Dad sits at his desk. "This will be fun!" he says.

"That's it!" says Dad. Dad is cross.

The model tilts and then - smash!

Just then, Sam and Tam rush in. Thud!

Cut out the sentences. Read and match to the correct pictures.

Book 13c - Sentence dictation

The   model   _____ _____ _____ _____ _____

_____ _____   _____ _____ _____ _____   -   _____ _____ _____ _____!

Offer the sentence below as dictation. Encourage the children to sound out the words as they spell them.

The model tilts and then - smash!

Book 13c - Free writing

Free writing with picture cues. This page can also be used for sentence dictation using sentences from the book.

High-frequency words: his, be, he, says, I, a, the, model, is

Book 13c - Sentence handwriting

Just then, Sam and Tam rush in. Thud!

The model tilts and then - smash!

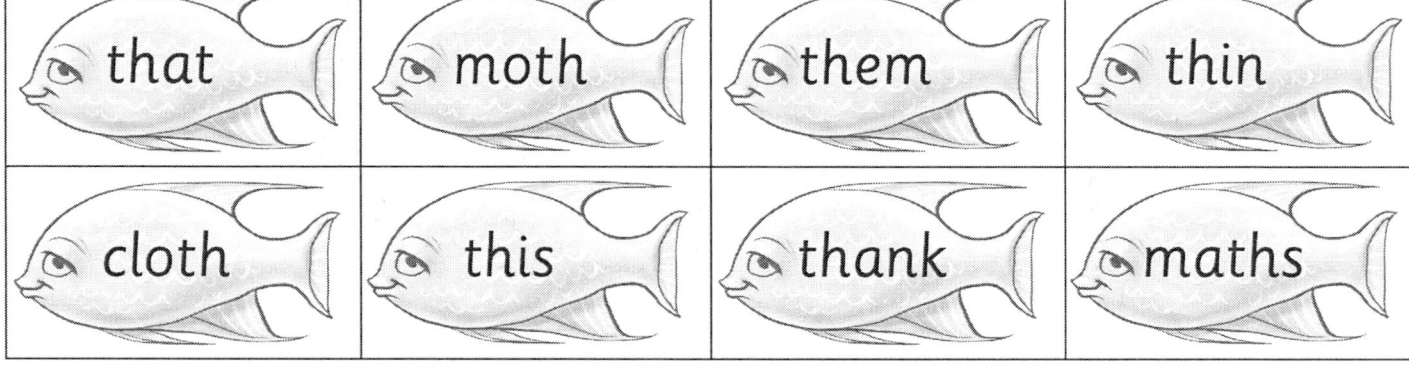

Book 13d - That's it!: th

'th' as in 'thin'

'th' as in 'this'

| that | moth | them | thin |
| cloth | this | thank | maths |

The spelling 'th' can represent two different sounds: 'th' as in 'thin' and 'th' as in 'this'. Read the words and listen to the 'th' sounds. Put the fish in the right fishing nets.

Book 13d - Retell the story

'That's It!'

This page can be photocopied onto card. Cut out these pictures for retelling the story or for children to make their own story. Can also be used to reinforce vocabulary.

Book 13d - Comprehension

Mum fixes up the shelves. "This is not bad!" she says.

This is Dad's den - in the shed.

"That's it!" says Dad. "I am fed up!"

Josh gets Dad. Dad thinks this is fun.

Cut out the sentences. Read and match to the correct pictures.

Book 13d - Sentence dictation

‗‗‗‗ ‗‗‗ ‗‗‗‗   ‗‗‗ ‗‗‗ ‗‗‗   ‗‗‗ ‗‗ ‗‗ .

‗‗‗‗‗‗‗ ‗‗‗ ‗‗‗‗   is   ‗‗‗ ‗‗ ‗‗ .

Offer the sentences below as dictation. Encourage the children to sound out the words as they spell them.

Josh gets Dad. This is fun.

Book 13d - Free writing

Free writing with picture cues. This page can also be used for sentence dictation using sentences from the book.

High-frequency words: says, I, the, she, shelves, is

Book 13d - Sentence handwriting

Josh gets Dad.
Dad thinks this is
fun.

This is Dad's den
.. in the shed!

Word handwriting

this

cloth

think

thin

Unit 13 - 4-in-a-row Game : th

thin	that	path	thanks	this
maths	path	them	cloth	then
Beth	thump	moth	think	bath
sloth	thank	moths	thin	that
moth	thanks	this	maths	path
Beth	thump	moth	think	then
thud	thin	than	them	cloth

Play with two sets of coloured counters. Two players take turns to read the word and put a counter on the word. The winner is the first to get four of his or her counters in a row. The winner places a counter on an ice cream. The game is played four times until all the ice creams are covered.

Word-building and spelling list

thin

that

then

moth

thud

them

thank

cloth

think

thump

A list of words from this Unit to be used for spelling practice. Photocopiable cards for word-building are included at the back of the workbook.

Reading and Writing Activities

Unit 14

Book 14a - The Clock: ck

c l o ___

s o ___

d u ___

t r u ___

Josh is playing with his toys. Can you fill in the sounds to write the words?

Book 14a - The Clock: ck

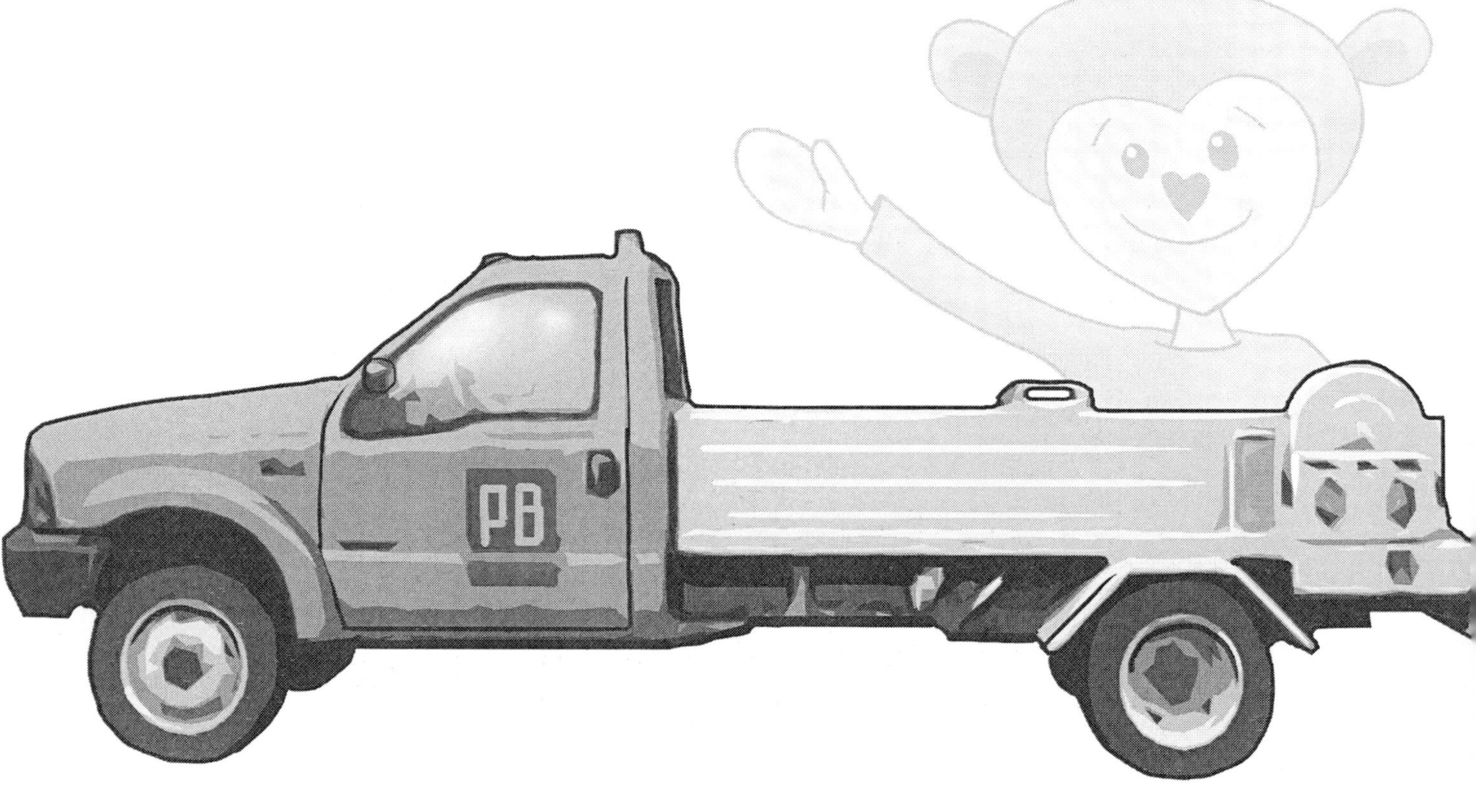

Josh is playing with his truck. Can you cut out the things that finish with a 'ck' spelling or 'k' sound in them and put them in his truck?

Book 14a - Retell the story

'The Clock'

This page can be photocopied onto card. Cut out these pictures for retelling the story or for children to make their own story. Can also be used to reinforce vocabulary.

Book 14a - Comprehension

At 12 o'clock, Josh has a snack.

At 6 o'clock, Mum checks the clock.

At 8 o'clock, the kids run to get the bus.

At 5 o'clock, Mum has a rest. Sh!

Cut out the sentences. Read and match to the correct pictures.

Book 14a - Sentence dictation

6 o'clock,

the   .

Offer the sentence below as dictation. Encourage the children to sound out the words as they spell them.

At 6 o'clock Mum checks the clock.

Book 14a - Free writing

Free writing with picture cues. This page can also be used for sentence dictation using sentences from the book.

High-frequency words: o'clock, the, to, is, his, has, a, have

Book 14a - Sentence handwriting

At 6 o'clock, Mum

checks the clock.

At 12 o'clock,

Josh has a snack.

Book 14b - The Back Pack: ck

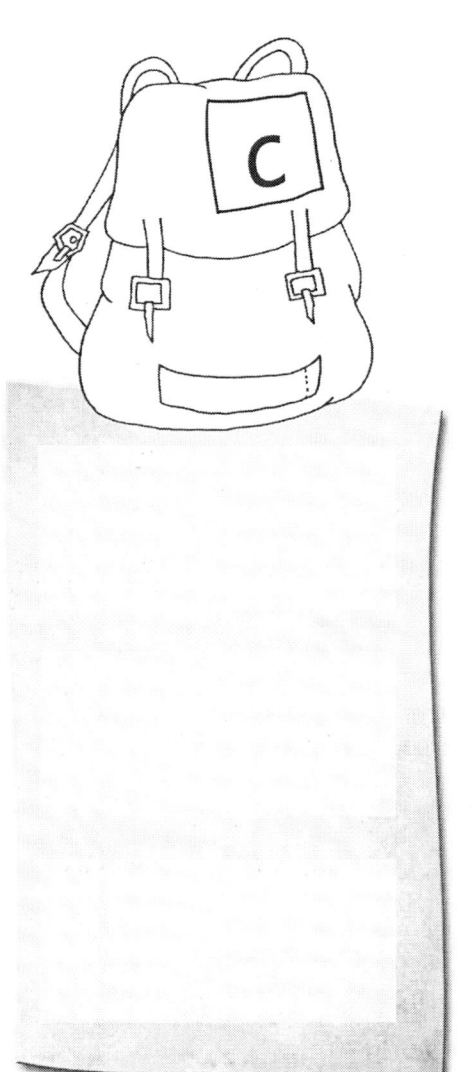 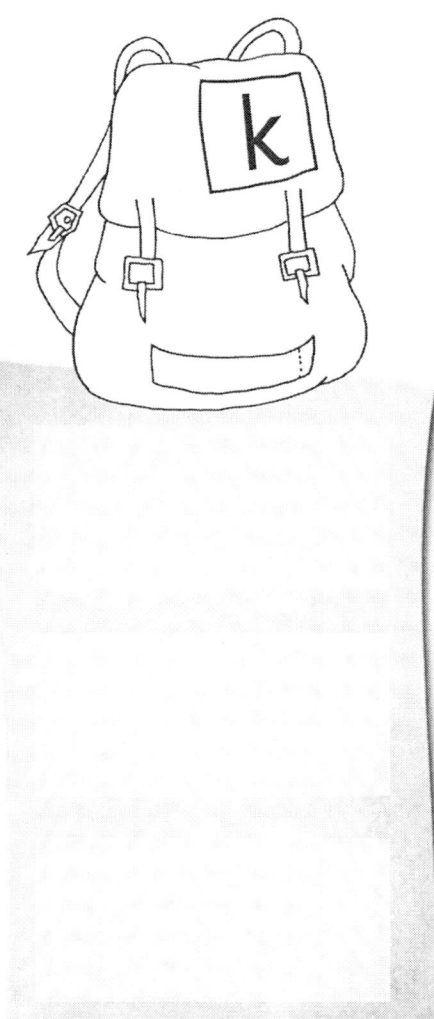 

duck	sock	can
kip	cot	kid
cup	Ken	lick

Viv is sorting words for her back pack.
Each bag shows one of the spellings of the 'k' sound.
Can you read and sort the cards?

Book 14b - Retell the story

'The Back Pack'

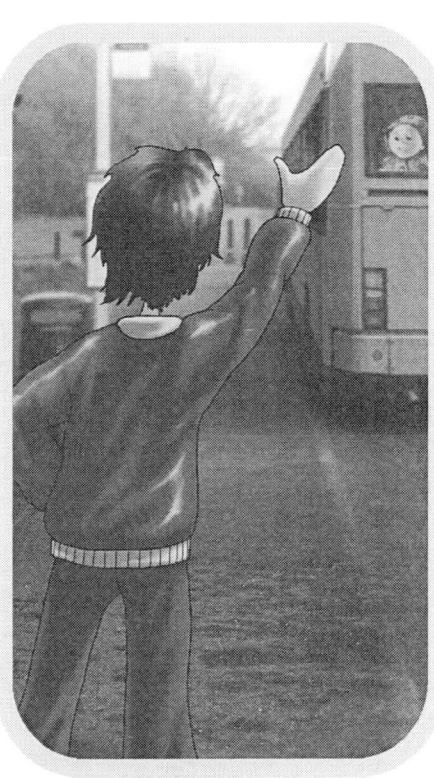

This page can be photocopied onto card. Cut out these pictures for retelling the story or for children to make their own story. Can also be used to reinforce vocabulary.

Book 14b - Comprehension

Viv packs a vest and socks.

The back pack is on the bench.

Viv packs a snack for the trip.

"Stop the bus! I have the back pack!" Mum yells.

Cut out the sentences. Read and match to the correct pictures.

Book 14b - Sentence dictation

" _____ _____ _____ you _____ _____ _____ _____

_____ _____ _____ _____ ?" _____ _____ _____ asks.

Offer the sentence below as dictation. Encourage the children to sound out the words as they spell them.

"Did you pack a snack?" Mum asks.

Book 14b - Free writing

Free writing with picture cues. This page can also be used for sentence dictation using sentences from the book.

High-frequency words: the, for, says, you, a, asks, is, have

Book 14b - Sentence handwriting

"Let's pack for the trip," says Mum.

"Did you pack a snack?" Mum asks.

Book 14c - Which Shall I Pick?: ck

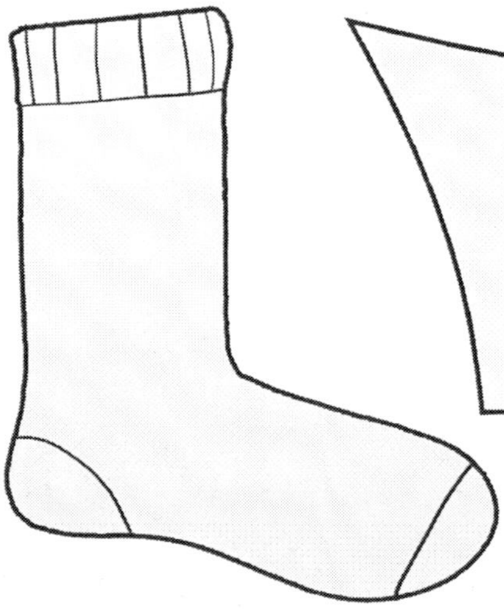

th i ___   s o ___

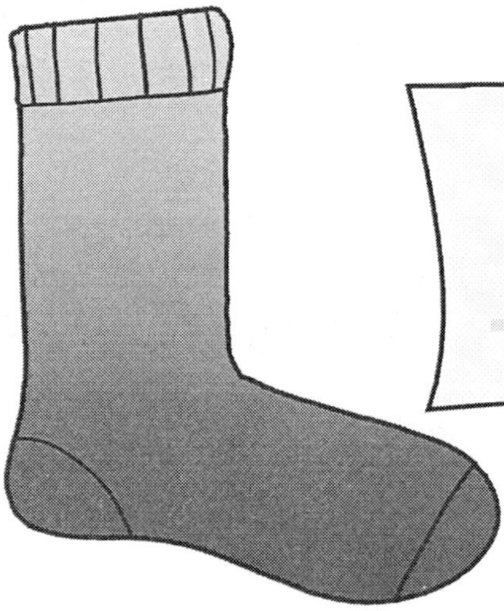

b l ___   s o ___

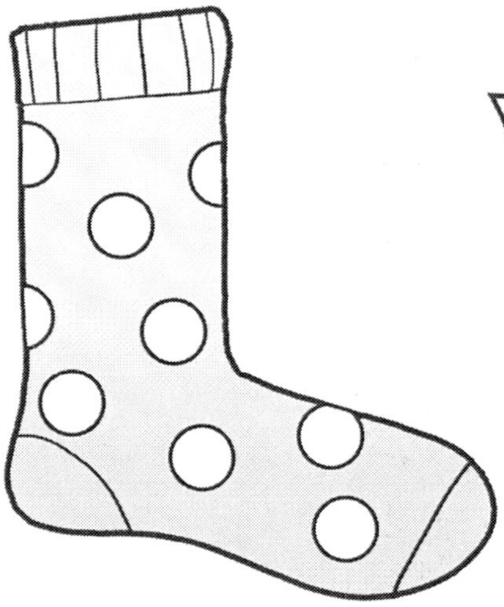

s o ___   w i th ___

Which shall I pick?
Can you fill in the missing sounds to finish the labels on the socks?

Book 14c - Retell the story

'Which Shall I Pick?'

This page can be photocopied onto card. Cut out these pictures for retelling the story or for children to make their own story. Can also be used to reinforce vocabulary.

Book 14c - Comprehension

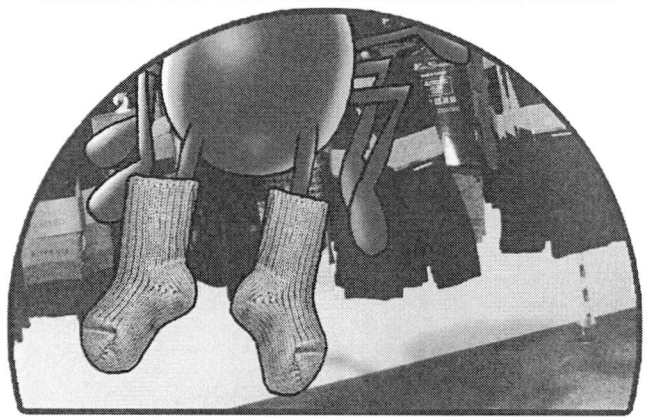

Jim put on the thick socks.

When Jim got cold, he went to the sock shop.

"Which socks shall I pick?"

"Shall I pick the black socks with red spots?"

Cut out the sentences. Read and match to the correct pictures.

Book 14c - Sentence dictation

"Which _____ _____ _____ _____

_____ _____ I put _____ _____ ?"

Offer the sentence below as dictation. Encourage the children to sound out the words as they spell them.

"Which socks shall I put back?"

Book 14c - Free writing

Free writing with picture cues. This page can also be used for sentence dictation using sentences from the book.

High-frequency words: cold, he, to, the, I, put

Book 14c - Sentence handwriting

When Jim got cold, he went to the sock shop.

"Which socks shall I put back?"

Book 14d - When Can I Get On?

whud

which

wheff

whib

whop

when

whip

whack

Rex is flying on the jet!
Can you colour in the clouds that have a real word on?

Book 14d - Retell the story

'When Can I Get On?'

This page can be photocopied onto card. Cut out these pictures for retelling the story or for children to make their own story. Can also be used to reinforce vocabulary.

Book 14d - Comprehension

Rex gets on the jet. Crash!	Rex gets cross and whacks his fist.
It is six o'clock. "When can I get on the jet?"	Rex is in shock. "Bad luck," says Jill.

Cut out the sentences. Read and match to the correct pictures.

Book 14d - Sentence dictation

_____ is _____ _____ . "

_____ ____ _____ ," says _____ _____ .

Offer the sentences below as dictation. Encourage the children to sound out the words as they spell them.

Rex is in shock. "Bad luck," says Jill.

 © Phonic Books Ltd 2012

Book 14d - Free writing

Free writing with picture cues. This page can also be used for sentence dictation using sentences from the book.

High-frequency words: I, the, asks, said

Book 14d - Sentence handwriting

At seven o'clock,

Rex gets on the jet.

Rex is in shock.

"Bad luck," says

Jill.

Word handwriting

Unit 14 - 4-in-a-row Game : ck

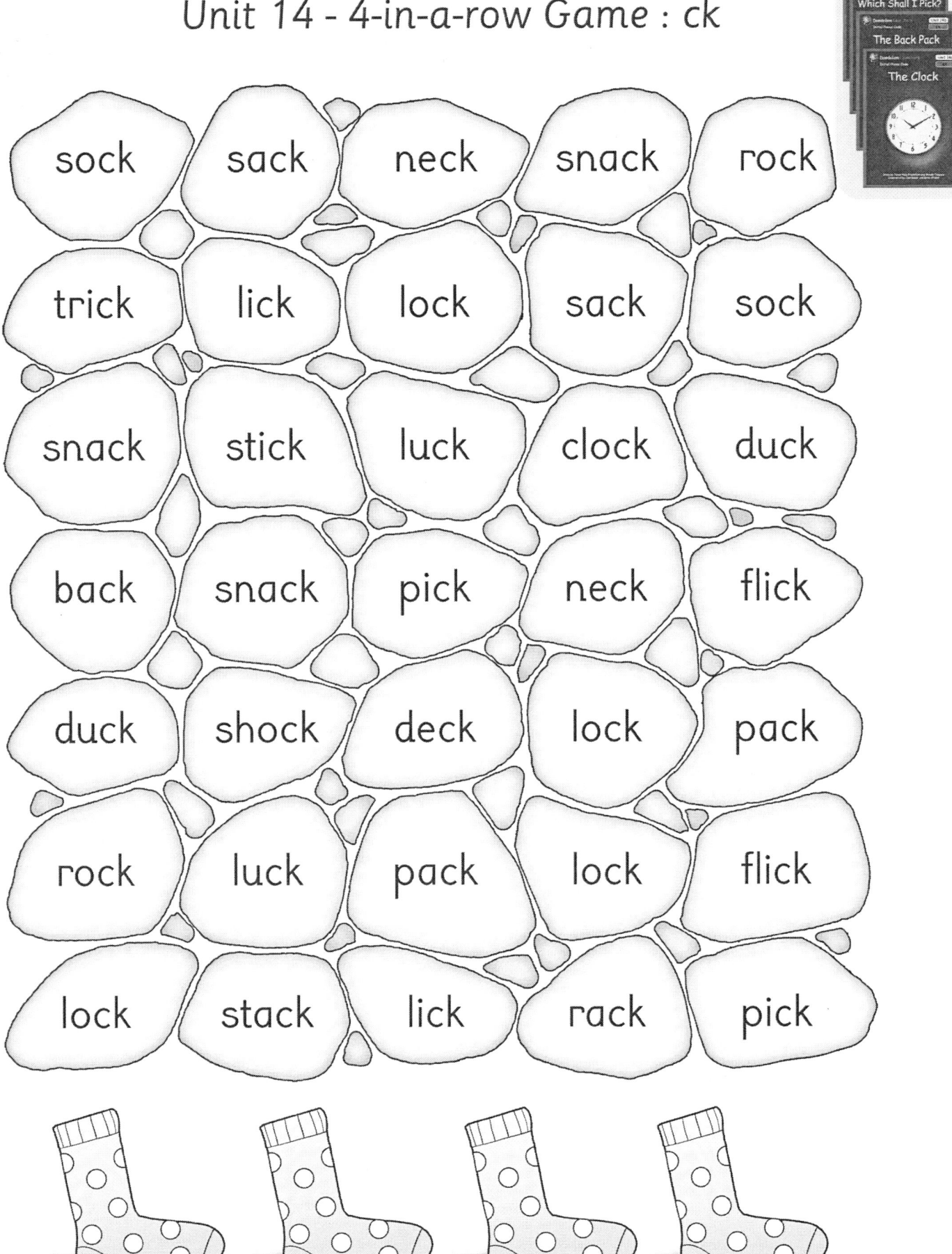

sock	sack	neck	snack	rock
trick	lick	lock	sack	sock
snack	stick	luck	clock	duck
back	snack	pick	neck	flick
duck	shock	deck	lock	pack
rock	luck	pack	lock	flick
lock	stack	lick	rack	pick

Play with two sets of coloured counters. Two players take turns to read the word and put a counter on the word. The winner is the first to get four of his or her counters in a row. The winner places a counter on a sock. The game is played four times until all the socks are covered.

Word-building and spelling list

ck	wh
sock	which
neck	whack
pack	when
kick	
luck	
snack	
flick	

A list of words from this Unit to be used for spelling practice. Photocopiable cards for word-building are included at the back of the workbook.

Reading and Writing Activities

Unit 15

Book 15a - Ding, Dong!: ng

w i ___

r i ___

s w i ___

k i ___

Sam has been hanging his favourite pictures.
Can you fill in the sounds to write the words?

Book 15a - Ding, Dong!: ng

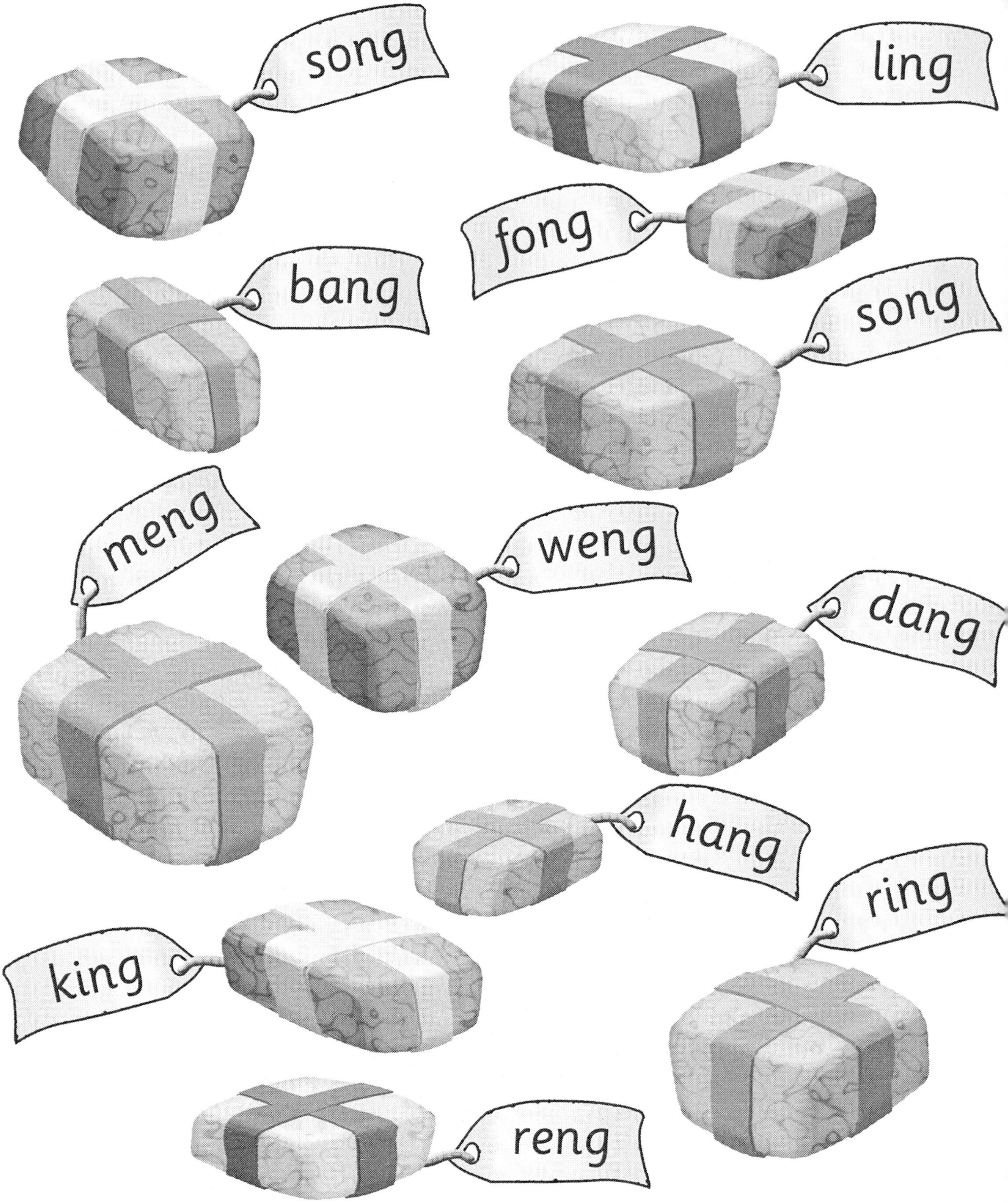

song

ling

fong

bang

song

meng

weng

dang

hang

king

ring

reng

Can you colour in the presents that are real words with a 'ng' spelling?
Which one has a ⬤ inside?

Book 15a - Retell the story

'Ding, Dong!'

This page can be photocopied onto card. Cut out these pictures for retelling the story or for children to make their own story. Can also be used to reinforce vocabulary.

Book 15a - Comprehension

Ding, dong, rings the bell.

"Can I have an egg?" Tam brings Sam an egg.

"Can I have a jug of milk?"

Tim and Sam sing Tam a song.

Cut out the sentences. Read and match to the correct pictures.

Book 15a - Sentence dictation

_____ _____ _____ _____ _____ _____

_____ _____ a _____ _____ .

Offer the sentence below as dictation. Encourage the children to sound out the words as they spell them.

Tim and Sam sing Tam a song.

Book 15a - Free writing

Free writing with picture cues. This page can also be used for sentence dictation using sentences from the book.

High-frequency words: is, the, I, have, a, of, happy birthday, to, you

Book 15a - Sentence handwriting

Ding, dong, rings
the bell.

"Sh! Stop that
song!
It's 5 o'clock!"

Book 15b - Spring: ng

ki____

wi____

stri____

swi____

ri____

Can you fill in the missing 'ng' sounds and draw a line to match the labels to the pictures on Sam's wall?

Book 15b - Retell the story

'Spring'

This page can be photocopied onto card. Cut out these pictures for retelling the story or for children to make their own story. Can also be used to reinforce vocabulary.

Book 15b - Comprehension

"Then I can sing too!" says Sam, "La, la, la…"

Red Bill sings at the top of his lungs.

"The sun is up. Let's sing a song!" says Red Bill.

Sam sits up. "Sh! Stop that song! It's 5 o'clock!"

Cut out the sentences. Read and match to the correct pictures.

Book 15b - Sentence dictation

"I can ___ ___ ___ a ___ ___ ___ !"

says ___ ___ ___ ___ ___ ___ .

Offer the sentence below as dictation. Encourage the children to sound out the words as they spell them.

"I can sing a song!" says Red Bill.

Book 15b - Free writing

Free writing with picture cues. This page can also be used for sentence dictation using sentences from the book.

High-frequency words: is, the, a, says, I, his, o'clock, of, too, branch

Book 15b - Sentence handwriting

It is spring. The sun is up but Sam is still in bed.

Red Bill sings at the top of his lungs.

Book 15c - Ting-A-Ling: ng

song

long

fling

hang

feng

bing

sting

swing

fang

weng

hong

reng

Quin is king of the dogs.

Can you colour in the bones that have a real word on them?

Book 15c - Retell the story

'Ting-A-Ling'

This page can be photocopied onto card. Cut out these pictures for retelling the story or for children to make their own story. Can also be used to reinforce vocabulary.

Book 15c - Comprehension

When Quin nods off, Ken fixes a bell on him.

"It's Quin, king of the dogs!" Quick, Ken, run!

Ken sits on a swing and thinks of a plan.

Quin is king of the dogs.

Cut out the sentences. Read and match to the correct pictures.

Book 15c - Sentence dictation

_____ _____ _____ is _____ _____ _____

of the _____ _____.

Offer the sentence below as dictation. Encourage the children to sound out the words as they spell them.

Quin is king of the dogs.

Book 15c - Free writing

Free writing with picture cues. This page can also be used for sentence dictation using sentences from the book.

High-frequency words: a, is, of, the, I, to, have, fixes, says

Book 15c - Sentence handwriting

151

Quin is king of the dogs.

"I have just the plan!" Ken springs off the swing.

Book 15d - The Strong Wind

quit

queb

quot

quilt

quish

quid

quip

qualg

quiz

quest

Dot is looking for leaves with 'qu' words on.
Cut out the cards with Dot on and stick her onto the leaves that have a real word with the 'qu' spelling.

Book 15d - Retell the story

'The Strong Wind'

This page can be photocopied onto card. Cut out these pictures for retelling the story or for children to make their own story. Can also be used to reinforce vocabulary.

Book 15d - Comprehension

Dot ran up a long stem.
Dot did not quit the song.

"I have spots. You do not!" Dot sang to Pip.

Dot felt a strong wind.
She hung from the stem.

The wind flung Dot in to the pond.

Cut out the sentences. Read and match to the correct pictures.

Book 15d - Sentence dictation

The _____ _____

_____ to the _____.

Offer the sentence below as dictation. Encourage the children to sound out the words as they spell them.

The wind flung Dot in to the pond.

Book 15d - Free writing

Free writing with picture cues. This page can also be used for sentence dictation using sentences from the book.

High-frequency words: I, have, you, do, to, he, said, the, a, she, yelled

Book 15d - Sentence handwriting

Pip got cross.
"Quit that song!"
he said.

The wind flung
Dot in to the pond.

Word handwriting

song

swing

quest

quit

Unit 15 - 4-in-a-row Game : 'ng' 'qu'

ring	song	spring	wing	king
long	bang	sting	Quin	sing
quit	king	quid	lung	long
hung	quit	long	king	bang
ring	song	king	hangs	quiz
wing	ring	sing	wing	sling
sting	wing	quit	spring	song

Play with two sets of coloured counters. Two players take turns to read the word and put a counter on the word. The winner is the first to get four of his or her counters in a row. The winner places a counter on a ring. The game is played four times until all the rings are covered.

Word-building and spelling list

ng	qu
ring	quiz
long	quit
bang	quest
hung	quilt
fling	
sprang	
hangs	

A list of words from this Unit to be used for spelling practice. Photocopiable cards for word-building are included at the back of the workbook.

Word-building cards

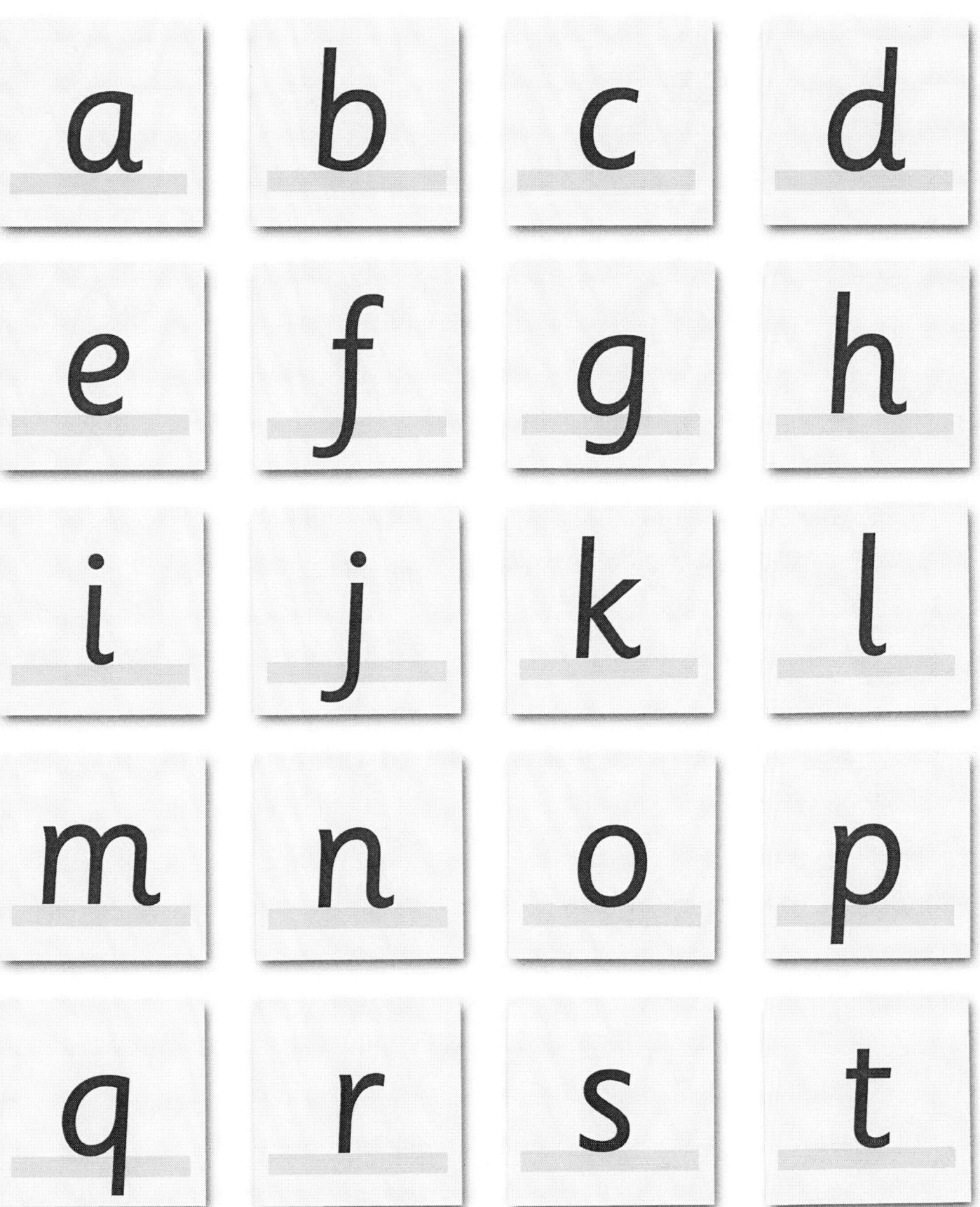

These cards can be photocopied onto card and used for word-building activities.

Word-building cards

u   v   w   x

y   z

ch   sh   th   ck

wh   ng   qu   a

e   i   o   u

These cards can be photocopied onto card and used for word-building activities.